Backpacks
and *Baguettes*

Coloring the World through Young Eyes

www.mascotbooks.com

Backpacks and Baguettes: Coloring the World through Young Eyes

For more information, please contact:
Mascot Books
620 Herndon Parkway, Suite 320
Herndon, VA 20170
info@mascotbooks.com

Library of Congress Control Number: 2020905254

CPSIA Code: PRV0620A
ISBN-13: 978-1-64543-287-6

Printed in the United States

To Paris

Backpacks and Baguettes

Coloring the World through Young Eyes

Sam Morrison
and **Angus Morrison**

Illustrated by
Marco Primo

Introduction

I'm Sam. Angus is my father. Good to meet you. I think traveling is important because it gives you a chance to experience other cultures and get out of your normal environment. It teaches you how other people's lives are different from your own—sometimes better, sometimes worse.

I've been lucky to travel a lot because my parents have chosen to work and live in other countries and because—like me—they believe in traveling. Some people like to spend their money on cars or watches or houses. That's fine. I just prefer to spend it on traveling. I also think you shouldn't keep these experiences only in your own head. You should share them with other people so they can learn, too.

We tried to tell our stories with words. We also used graffiti and street art that I've seen around the world because they are better than most post cards. They're real. But I don't know what all the graffiti means, so keep that in mind.

My father and I say that if we had a lot of money, like if we won the lottery, we'd buy airline tickets or seats on a sailboat for kids who don't have the ability to travel. That way, they would understand that there are worlds out there they may have never imagined— worlds that are different from the ones they live in every day, worlds they may want to explore and make their own one day.

Brussels, Belgium

- Belgium shares a border with four countries. Can you name them?[1]
- Belgium exports more chocolate than any other country in the world.
- French fries were invented in Belgium, not France.

The guy who invented the saxophone is from Brussels. It's also Tintin's hometown. I have a lot of his books. What I like about him is that adults tend to underestimate him because he's a boy. I think that's his special power. One of my favorite Tintin books is *The Black Island*—the one where he's in Scotland and has to battle a gorilla in a castle.

Brussels is also home to something called the European Union. It's basically a bunch of countries that started working together after the Second World War to prevent themselves from shooting each other anymore.

One thing I've learned on my travels is that the way people act and think is often related to the size of their country and its reputation in the world. For

1   See the back of the book for answers.

example, Belgium is small—about the size of the U.S. state New Jersey. Like Switzerland, another small country, Belgium is not big enough to boss other countries around. They have to figure out ways to be more clever than their bigger neighbors. It reminds me of when I play soccer. I'm small for my age, so I can't use my weight to move people off the ball like other guys. My coach last year, Khalid, is also a small guy, and he played professional soccer in France. He always tried to teach me to use my brain instead of my body. I sometimes just wish I was bigger, but I know what he means.

One of the things I like doing in Brussels is eating *frites*. They're french fries, but they are fried twice. I like it best when you get a warm cone of them wrapped in paper on a cold day. In Great Britain, where my granny and grandad are from, they used to serve fish and chips in newspapers that people had already read. My granny and grandad said the ink from the newspaper added flavor. The Belgians have way more sauces for their frites than ketchup or mustard. Mayonnaise is a normal dipping sauce there. You can also have something called *Andalouse*, which tastes like spaghetti sauce. There's *Pili-Pili*, which is quite hot. So is *Samourai*. And there's *Americain* which has onions, tomatoes, cayenne pepper, butter, and sometimes a liquor called cognac made in France that my grandad likes to drink after a good dinner.

I also like going to the Grand Place in Brussels. It's one of the best places in all of Europe, with gold leaf buildings and medieval architecture. Every couple of years they make a flower carpet covering the entire place.

My mummy grew up in Brussels even though she is British. It's where my mummy and daddy met a long time ago. It's a special place for them. When we are there together, we meet up with friends, eat steak frites with Béarnaise sauce, and go for walks in Tervuren park. My friend, Louis, fell in the pond there once when we were younger. We had to fish him out.

What impresses me most about the kids in Belgium is that they are super good at languages. Most speak some combination of French, Flemish, and English. Other kids can speak all of those, plus German. Flemish is like Dutch but they sometimes use different words and their accent sounds different. A lot of Flemish words sound sort of English. For example, do you know the word for someone who talks too much? *Babbelkous.* How about the word for matches? *Lucifers.*

Belgian French is pretty much the same as in France, but Belgians count differently. In France, once you count to 70 or 90 it gets complicated. It's hard for English speakers to get used to it, but for the French it's just normal. So, for example, if you want to say 75 in French, you say *soixante-quinze*, or 60+15. That's a lot to think about in your head just to say a number. And 95 is *quatre-vingt-quinze*, or 4x20+15. Belgian French is more logical for an English speaker. You say *septante-cinq*, for 75 and *nonante-cinq* for 95.

Italy

- More than 30 percent of Italians don't use the Internet.
- Tomatoes weren't originally from Italy. Can you guess where they were from?[2]
- The wolf is the unofficial national animal of Italy.

One of my grandmothers is Italian-American. I call her *nonna*. Her father was from near Florence. My nonna smiles a lot and has curly hair, like our cousins in Tuscany whom we visit often. In Italy, people use their hands and talk about food.

Another thing you notice in Italy is that parents bring their children with them to a lot of things. Not every country is like that. On Sundays families go for walks together and then get *gelato*. That means ice cream in Italian. Italians also talk to people in other cars while they are driving. Well, they actually yell more than talk. I can't really tell what they are saying, but it's clear that they aren't very happy.

---

2   See the back of the book for answers.

I have many good memories of Italy—too many to put all of them in this book—so I'll focus on only two of them: Tuscany and Sicily.

Tuscany has rolling hills like the ones in North Carolina where my nonna lives now. A lot of artists and inventors came from Tuscany. My favorite is probably Leonardo da Vinci because he was constantly inventing. I was lucky to go to the mansion where he died in France. Some of my cousins live near the village of Vinci in Italy where he was from.

One time in Tuscany, my father took me mushroom hunting. Some of our cousins are real experts. They know which mushrooms to pick and eat. That's important because if you get a bad mushroom, it can kill you. What's interesting when you mushroom hunt in Italy is that people are very protective of the places where they find them. We take a neighbor named Carlo who is in his eighties and has picked mushrooms in the same places his entire life. My father says he has a mushroom GPS in his head.

Porcini are like the king of the mushroom world for Italians. You usually find them under trees, and you need a special tool to get them. One side has a curved knife, while the other side has a little brush to take off the dirt. You don't pull the mushrooms out of the ground because they won't grow back next year if you do. You want to cut the stem right where it comes out of the ground. You then put your mushrooms in a basket that you carry around with you. And here's the clever part: You put a towel or a newspaper over the top of the mushrooms so it looks like the bottom of the basket. That way, when snoopy people in the forest ask you, "How is the mushroom hunting today?" and try to sneak a peek into your basket, you say to them, "Oh, not very good, only a couple. See?"

The best part of mushroom hunting is the eating. Our cousin, Licia, usually had everyone over to her house, and we cooked the mushrooms up in different ways. Some are fried, some are cooked and crushed into a paste to put on top of bread, others are made into a soup, and others are made into a sauce to go over pasta. It's an all-day thing. Licia is no longer with us. We miss her and the magical things she did with mushrooms.

Sicily is an island in the south of Italy and is very different from the north. In fact, the Sicilian version of Italian uses different words and phrases than in Tuscany. Lots of people from different places have lived in Sicily: Greeks, Romans, Arabs, French, Spaniards, Germans, and even the Vikings!

Because so many different people settled in Sicily, their food is interesting. They like to mix meat with fruit, for example. When they make meatballs, like I do with my nonna, they add raisins and pine nuts. I also like something called *arancini*. It's like a fried rice ball with ham and cheese inside. And I like cannolis. Who doesn't, right?

Sicily has a huge volcano called Mt. Etna. My mother and father and I climbed up it one day. It's interesting because the land is all black where the lava has rolled over the Earth. It takes everything in its path. We even saw part of a house that was buried by the lava. At night, you can see fire coming out of the top of Mt. Etna.

Sicily had problems once upon a time. That's why people like my great-grandmother's family had to move to America. But it seems better now.

Zurich, Switzerland

- People in Switzerland vote directly for their leaders. They vote more often than any country in the word. They vote on things like school hours and changing bus routes.
- Switzerland has the world's longest tunnel: the Gotthard Base railway tunnel. It's 57 km long.
- Along with Vatican City, Switzerland is the only other country in the world to have a square flag—a red square with a white cross.

You can spell Zurich six different ways. The Swiss speak German in this city, but in other parts of Switzerland, they speak French and Italian. They even speak a very old language called Romansh, which was brought to Switzerland by the Romans when they entered a valley called Engadin. My father does cross-country ski marathons there.

Zurich is mostly about banks, chocolate, watches, and Roger Federer who lives there, but was born in Basel. Zurich has a great lake. In the summer, it is the color of blueberry juice. In the winter, when it's cold, parts of it freeze, and you can skate on it. We did that once with our friends, Nadja and Lyle.

I love a restaurant in Zurich called the Zeughauss-keller. They have something called the *Burgermeister Schwert,* or "the mayor's sword." Two people have to eat it. It's pieces of beef on a long sword with garlic and curry sauce. Mmm.

Switzerland has been a neutral country during wartime for 190 years. That's because the mountains make it very hard to invade and because all the men are in the army part time.

The Swiss have a lot of rules. My father told me once that a man in a car told him off because he forgot to get off his bike before he went on a crosswalk. Swiss children don't seem to have a lot of stress. That might have something to do with the fact that Swiss cities rank in the top ten best places to live. Kids have access to clean air and the Alps, which are a part of everyone's life in Switzerland, both in the winter and the summer. Once when we were in the Alps, we camped along a lake. In the morning, three men woke us up by playing long horns shaped like smoking pipes called *alpen-horns.* No wonder people in Switzerland are happy. If I was woken up like that every day, I'd be happy, too.

Scarborough, England

- It is believed Danish Vikings arrived in Scarborough in the tenth century.
- During the Middle Ages, Scarborough had a big trading market that lasted forty-five days. People would come from all over Europe.
- Scarborough has the lowest pay in Britain with an average salary of just £19,925, compared to a national average of £28,442.

Scarborough sits in a harbor on the North Sea and has always been a fishing and trading town. There's an old song about it called, "Are You Going to Scarborough Fair?" Ask your parents—they'll know about it.

A Roman castle sits above the city. I can see it from my room at my granny's when I fall asleep. It's not really a castle—it's more of a stone fort, but the local people call it a castle. It was the last Roman light-house before getting to Scotland, which they used to call Caledonia. Before the Romans, there were people living on this cliff since the Iron Age. That's the time when they started making swords out of metal. My father sometimes takes me to the castle to wander, get blown around by the North Sea wind, and fight each other with wooden swords. You can see for miles and miles from the top of the castle. Sometimes when we are lucky, we can see seals swimming or even porpoises. I try to imagine what it was like to be a Roman soldier in the castle. It must have been super cold. They must have always been standing around a fire.

One of the things I notice in Scarborough is that there seem to be a lot of people with tattoos—both women and men. My English granny is from Scarborough, and I have several cousins who were born in Scarborough. Many of them don't live there anymore, but we still meet up in town. My granny and grandad also live there part of the year.

People in Scarborough talk a lot about being "hard," meaning tough. They are kind of hard on the outside but soft on the inside. I know what they mean by hard, though. In the middle of winter, when teenagers go out shopping, they sometimes wear nothing more than a t-shirt.

I think their hardness must come from the fact that Scarborough had a lot of Vikings in it once upon a time. They used to sail over from Denmark or Norway, beat up all the local people, and burn their houses until people paid them money, which they called the *danegeld*. Then they came back a few years later to do it all over again. In fact, people who live in Scarborough don't look like other English people. They look more like Scandinavians.

At Christmas time, there is a big soccer game on the beach between the fisherman and the firemen. The match has been a tradition for more than one hundred years. We always go and watch. There's a man who sells hot chestnuts in brown paper bags. I like how they smell. At the end of the game, they usually drag one of the players into the North Sea, which is very cold. And on Boxing Day, the day after Christmas, many young people go surfing in wet suits.

Fish and chips are considered very good in Scarborough. We eat them at the beach. My granny eats them with something called "mushy peas" which are like regular peas but crushed up into a paste. I don't like them very much.

I fish with my father on the stone pier in the North Sea and I watch the fishermen unload their fish. One thing I've learned in my travels is that cities and towns go through good times and bad times, just like people. Scarborough is like that.

Mosset, France

- This region of France, called Languedoc-Roussillon, has three times the number of vineyards as Bordeaux.
- In the 20th century, about one in every ten bottles of wine in the world was produced in this region.
- This is the second hottest region in France after Corsica. Sun lizards love it here.

My granny and grandad live half the year in England and the other half in a hill-village in the south of France called Mosset. It's on the border with Spain. My granny and grandad are retired. Retirement means you get to do what you want and no one bosses you around or makes you do things you don't want to do. My other grandparents are also retired. They say it means every day is Saturday. I can't wait to be retired, but it's a long way away.

If you hike to the top of some of the mountains in Mosset, you can see both the spine of the Pyrenees mountain range and the Mediterranean Sea. There are only about two hundred people who live in Mosset.

It's an ancient village that has seen many armies and kings passing through.

Mosset has a lot of characters—like Pierre. He used to be a surgeon in Paris but grew up in Mosset. He and my father are close. They cook snails together and have coffee at the café. Pierre had a dog named Nelson. He used to sometimes feed him Camembert cheese. Pierre drives around in a banged-up car that a horse kicked when it was angry one day.

José is another one. He is originally from Chile in South America but had to leave because the president of the country at the time didn't like people like him. José was called a Communist. I don't know what that means entirely, but it seems to scare some people. France said he could live in Mosset instead of Chile.

Some villages in France and other parts of Europe are considered "dead" if all the young people have moved away. The French call these villages a *carte postale,* or postcard, because they are beautiful to look at but are a bit boring. Mosset is not a carte postale because it has a school with about twenty-five children. In the summer I play soccer with some of the kids. They ask me questions about where I'm from and what my life is like, and I ask them about their lives. For kids in

Mosset, the size of the village probably means different things to them. It's probably like the story of the three bears. For some kids, the village is too small, and they'll want to leave one day. For others, it's too big, and for some, it's probably just right.

One thing that is interesting about Mosset that you may not see in a lot of other places is the bar. It's not just a bar. It's a bar plus a restaurant plus a canteen. The canteen is for the school. The village's agreement is that whomever the chef is at the bar/restaurant is also responsible for making lunch for the children. The teachers line the children up at lunchtime, and they all walk down the main road of the village, which is only about six feet wide. You should see what the chef makes for the kids! They have things like veal or steak from the cows that are raised around the village with potatoes topped off with local cheese. Other times they have quiche with local vegetables or chicken with roasted potatoes and chicken fat. It's way better than what they feed you for lunch in America. They are lucky children.

My granny has a garden on the hill above the village. She plants what English people call *courgettes* (zucchini), *aubergines* (eggplant), carrots, lettuce, peppers, corn, cucumbers, and strawberries. When I lived in Paris, we would drive down in the spring and help her plant her garden. Then we would eat it later in the summer when we visited. I like eating things that I plant. Now that I live back in the U.S., we don't have a garden. But I still get to eat from my granny's garden when we visit. There's also a big fig tree that makes shade. We sit under it in the evening when the sun is going down over the mountains. My mummy and daddy and granny and grandad have wine; I have Orangina, or water. Some of the villagers make crêpes out of the figs. They fry them up in butter and add local honey. It's one of my father's favorite dishes.

When the sun goes down, my father and I often camp in the garden. It's nice to sleep under the stars with the smell of the vegetables. When we wake up, we get to watch the sun rise over a big mountain called Canigou. My father has climbed Canigou several times. At the top, there is a cross like the one that Jesus was nailed to that the Catalan put up there. It's made of iron. I don't know how they got it way up there. I haven't climbed it yet with my father, but I've seen pictures. Canigou is a spiritual mountain for the Catalan people. Who are they?

The Catalan people have a long history. I can't tell you the whole story here—and I don't even know all of it—but what I do know is that they've always lived in the Pyrenees mountains. Sometimes their bosses were the Romans, sometimes the Arabs, and sometimes the Spanish or the French. Nowadays, the Catalan people live on both sides of the Spanish and French border. They like to make these human pyramid things where they stand on each other's shoulders. They eat a lot of sausages and anchovies, tomatoes, and aubergine. And they have a dessert similar to crème brûlée—if you've ever had that—only they call it *Crema Catalana*. I think it's better.

You can hear three languages in Mosset: French, Spanish, and Catalan—which is like a combination of French and Spanish. I like Mosset. It moves at a slower speed.

Marrakesh, Morocco

- Morocco is about the same size as the state of California.
- The money in Morocco is called *Dirham*.
- Experts think that Morocco is the home to the oldest university in the world. It's in a town called Res and is called Al-Qarawiyyin. It was founded in 859 AD.

You know how you have five senses—sight, smell, taste, touch, and hearing? You use all of them in Marrakesh. The sense you use the most in this city is probably smell because they have a lot of spices. And everything feels red because of the red earth and red walls around the city.

If you go to Marrakesh, you have to go to the market, which is called a *souk*. But be careful because it's like a maze. It's dark and crowded. I almost got lost there with my parents. We were trying to find a café that was on the top floor of a building. That's where people go to see around the market—the top floors of buildings. A teenage boy offered to guide us to the café for a little money. He knew exactly where to go. From the café, we could see into some enclosed gardens called *riads*.

In the market square, I watched a guy with a flute charm a cobra. That was crazy! One night, we went to a place where ladies in dresses that showed their bellies shook their hips. They do it while you're eating. One lady danced really close to me and brushed part of her sleeve on my face. I was a bit embarrassed, but people clapped for me.

Another thing about Marrakesh is when it is prayer time, a man sings in Arabic into loud speakers so everyone in the city can hear it. I like it. It sounds exotic.

Moroccan food is delicious. They eat something called *couscous,* which is like little pasta balls. They put anything on it—fish, meat, or vegetables. They also eat a kind of pie called *pastilla,* which has chicken, onions, dates, pistachios, and a lot of spices like saffron and turmeric. I can't eat it because I'm allergic to nuts, but my father loves it. He said it reminds him of when he rented a room from a Moroccan family in Brussels when he was just out of university. He said the family was hospitable to him. He was working a lot, and when he came home at night, there would be a knock on his door. When he opened it, a steaming bowl of couscous would be sitting on a chair. When he was done eating it, he would put it back on the chair, and the family's children would take it away. It was an interesting arrangement. They also let him kill a chicken during Ramadan.

I don't know if you know this, but one thing I learned in Morocco is that drinking hot tea when it's hot outside helps you cool down by sweating. Moroccans drink mint tea all the time. They take a boiling pot of water and put a handful of fresh mint leaves in there with about sixteen cubes of sugar. When they serve it to you, you can tell how much they like you by how high they hold the pot over the glass as they pour the tea. The more they like you, the higher they hold the pot. They held it really high for us.

Moroccan children smile a lot. Their language, Arabic, can sound angry to someone who doesn't understand it, but usually they are not angry. They are just talking. Moroccan boys like soccer. They were very proud of a famous Moroccan player who was considered the best African player in Europe. He was called "The Black Pearl." I never saw the Black Pearl play. In my lifetime, I think the best African player is Mo Salah. He's from Egypt and plays for one of my favorite teams, Liverpool.

One fact that I learned while in Morocco is that it was the first country in the world to recognize the United States after the war of independence from Great Britain.

South Africa

- South Africa has three capital cities: Cape Town, Pretoria, and ... for extra points guess what the third is.[3]
- South Africa has eleven languages.
- The springbok is the national animal.

Africa smells like grass and animals—like it's been there forever. I liked waking up to Africa when we were on a safari there. We usually woke at 5:30 in the morning, when the animals finished their night shift. That's when animals in the wild do their work—sort of the opposite of humans. Our guide, Vincent, would make us cups of tea that we would drink with a South African hard biscuit called *rusk*.

I grew to like Vincent a lot. He let me sit right behind him in the Jeep. He'd give me a blanket to keep me warm in the chilly morning air, and he let me watch him clean his rifle, which he kept in the front seat with him. He never let it out of his sight. Vincent had what

3   See answer in the back of the book.

they call "bush eyes." It means his eyes have adjusted to spotting animals in the wild in a way that city eyes can't do. He would point at things and joke with me saying, "The lion is right there. How come you can't see that? You have younger eyes than me. If he was any closer, he'd get you."

We sometimes had lunch with Vincent. We would eat meat from the animals like impala or guinea fowl. We also had something called *biltong*, which is a South African version of beef jerky.

Vincent told us about his family. He came from a tribe where men could have more than one wife. He said he preferred to only have one because it was too tiring to have more. He also told us stories about how sad it was to see animals being poached. I could tell it made him angry. He said there was a well-known guy in China who had cancer and claimed that the horns from rhino could cure it. He was so well known that poachers began to increase the number of rhinos they killed. Six months later, the man died of cancer.

Vincent also showed us a refuge for certain animals that had been adopted from other parts of the world. The saddest ones for me were the lions. They had a couple of lions who had come from circuses in Eastern

Europe. They had been badly mistreated and seemed to go back and forth between being scared and angry. I'd feel the same way if I were them.

In the evenings, we would sit around the camp fire. My parents would have tea or a drink and chat with a few of the South Africans. I would listen. I like just listening when people are sharing stories. They sometimes think that I'm not paying attention, but I am. They talked about difficulties between white and black people in South Africa. And they talked about crime. Things were getting violent when we were there. Some South Africans were getting angry about immigrants coming from other African countries and trying to work in the country. The king of a tribe called the Zulus was reported to have told foreigners to pack their bags and go. A few days later, a foreigner was killed by some men in Johannesburg just because he was a foreigner.

I don't understand stuff like that. Refugees don't want to have to move from their country, but they sometimes have to for a lot of reasons. I learned something about refugees when I lived in Paris. We lived there when refugees were coming from places in the Middle East, like Syria. They lived under the bridges in Paris. My school class made sandwiches, which my father would sometimes deliver to them. He met a fifteen-year-old boy who had walked to Paris from Afghanistan! I can't imagine what it's like to be a refugee.

Israel

- Israel is the only country in the world that has more trees today than it had fifty years ago.
- Israel has more museums per capita than any other country. It even has one that is under water.
- You know when people call and leave a message at your house on the answering machine? That technology was invented in Israel.

New York is about money; Hollywood is about movies; Israel is all about religion. You feel it when you are there.

We stayed in Tel Aviv with Jewish friends who I went to school with in Paris—Ella, Tzofia, and Arielle. They have lemon trees outside their house. We made lemonade. Israel has great fruit. When we arrived at their place, they said they were sorry, but they forgot to tell us that we had to go to something called a *bris*. I didn't know what a bris was, but I would soon find out.

We went to a Jewish place called a *shul*. It's like a church, but the women and men sit in separate sections. They gave my father and me a little hat that we had to wear on our heads. I sat behind a man with a really big head. There was singing and praying, and then they brought a baby to the front on a pillow. I couldn't see very well, but then the big-headed man moved to the right, and that's when I saw it. The man holding the baby—I think the grandfather—looked down at the baby and then up at the ceiling with a pained face as another man with some tools worked on the baby, who cried. Afterwards, people clapped and were happy, and we went downstairs for a big meal of different breads, hummus, vegetables, and cakes. There was a courtyard with other boys wearing the same little hat on their heads that I had. We played soccer. My father told me what a bris was all about later on. It must hurt.

One day, we took the bus from Tel Aviv to Jerusalem. They are very different cities. Tel Aviv has a beach and super fresh food. Jerusalem is old and serious. It's considered a holy city by Christians, Muslims, and Jews, who all have been fighting over it forever. We had to go on a Sunday because Jewish people take off Friday and Saturday. Many people don't use any electricity or drive on those days. Our friends in Tel Aviv don't. They make their food and coffee before Friday evening.

Some people have boys called *shabbos goy* that come over to turn on the electricity.

It was the first day after the Jewish holiday. The first thing I noticed on the bus was that we were the only riders without guns. The bus was full of Israeli soldiers going back to their jobs. Israel has men and women soldiers. Men serve three years; women serve two. Every solider has to carry a gun, even when they are off duty. They carry them at cafés, restaurants—even at the beach. It's odd to see people in bathing suits with rifles slung over their backs.

In Jerusalem, we visited a big stone wall where Jewish people pray and cry and stick pieces of paper in the cracks.

We also went to the church built on the site where they say Jesus was crucified and came back to life. I didn't know what to think of the place. It's a church, but some people treat it and other holy sites as if they were celebrity houses in Hollywood. In this church there are lots of different Christians who fight over which part of the church is theirs. And people in the church were sort of pushy. They elbowed and shoved each other.

One place where there was a lot of shoving was a stone where they say Jesus' body was laid out after he was crucified. Old ladies took towels out of their plastic bags and rubbed them on the stone. They didn't seem to care who was in their way, even children. I don't think Jesus would be impressed.

Sri Lanka

- People eat with their hands in Sri Lanka. That's why restaurants there have sinks that you can use to wash your hands before and after eating. No one wants curry fingers.
- Kids play a game where you tie a bread bun to a string and try to eat it with your hands tied behind your back.
- Lipton tea started in Sri Lanka back in the 1860s. People here like tea with milk and lots of sugar.

Sri Lanka used to be called Serendipity by people from Arabia and Persia. It is just below India. It looks like a tear drop. For many years it was also known as Ceylon. Sri Lanka had the first female prime minister in the world.

The people are super friendly. They put a lot of spices in their food—even more than in India. A lot of tea and cinnamon comes from Sri Lanka. Cinnamon looks nothing like the brown powder we put on our oatmeal. It's a green leaf.

Buddhist monks walk around Sri Lanka in colorful robes. When I was there, my parents took me to a turtle rehabilitation center on the same beach where the 2004 tsunami hit the coast. It killed many thousands of people, including 1,700 passengers on a train. We went to the place where they buried the dead, which was sad. We also went to a sanctuary for baby elephants that had lost their mothers.

By far the best part about Sri Lanka was riding around in a tuk tuk. It's the best way to get around. It was a bit scary because the driver wove in and out of traffic. He laughed because he knew he was scaring us, but I loved it. From the tuk tuk, I got a sense of what it's like to live in Sri Lanka every day. I saw people waiting for buses. I saw children coming home from school. And stray dogs. There are a lot of dogs walking around in Sri Lanka.

On the weekend, my father took me to a market where they were chopping up tuna, dolphin, and sharks. A man with no front teeth and a big knife and a bloody t-shirt smiled at me as he cut the head off one of the fish. There was a lot of yelling and it stank, but it was exciting.

One of the funniest things about Sri Lanka is that instead of nodding when people mean to agree, they shake their head back and forth, which can be confusing. Another curious thing was at the airport in Colombo. You see people leaving with refrigerators and TVs. They buy them there when they are returning from somewhere else. It's cheaper.

The children in Sri Lanka are very different from me or the children that I knew in Paris—and the ones I know now in Washington. They have lived through a lot—wars, tsunamis, and poverty. Some children don't get enough to eat or have access to doctors. Some had their parents killed in the civil war, and they were left to carry on for themselves. Some girls are forced to be married before they are eighteen. They say you should try to put yourself in other people's shoes, but it's hard for me to imagine these things.

Mauritius

- One of the rarest stamps in the world comes from Mauritius. It's called the Blue Mauritius Stamp. Some are worth more than one million euros each.
- You might think that a lot of countries are named after people, but that's not really the case. Mauritius was, though. It was named after a Dutch prince named Maurits van Nassau.
- Mauritius was the only known place where the Dodo bird lived.

Mauritius is in the middle of the Indian Ocean between Africa and India. They speak English, French, and Creole. Creole is like French, but they use some different words. For example, instead of saying, "Comment allez-vous?" (How are you?), they say, "Ki mayer." And when they reply, instead of saying "Ça va or ça va bien," (I'm well), they say "Mo byen, mersi." And their Creole is different from others spoken around the world like in Louisiana or Haiti.

My father tells me that Mauritius is like Sicily—everyone has passed through it. First it was the Arabs, then the Portuguese, the Dutch, the French, and finally, the British. The people living there now are Hindu, Tamil, Muslim, Chinese, and European. They all seem to get along, unlike other places I have been where people come from different backgrounds. Each of these people brought recipes to the island from their home countries. It's the sort of place where you can have Indian food for breakfast, African food for lunch, and Chinese food for dinner.

The people of Mauritius are pretty relaxed. You see them on the beach having parties or watching the sun go down, which is a big deal there. Children in school uniforms are always laughing and saying hi to each other. You also sometimes see men driving slowly on their bikes with big bushels of sugar cane attached to the back. Even they look happy, although I can imagine picking sugar cane is not easy.

We went to the market in Port Louis, the capital. They have all kinds of fruit and spices that they say cure sicknesses that people have, like diabetes and nervousness. There's even a town on the other side of the island that's called Pamplemousse, which means grapefruit in French.

People eat and visit at the market and buy things that they need for their houses, just like any market in the world. That's what I like about markets— they bring people out of their houses, and the people talk and share stories about their week. Some people play games at the market. I saw some men playing a dice game. You know what the dice were made of? Sugar cubes.

People also go to the market to taste different foods. My father fell in love with a dish called *poisson salé*, or salted fish. My father said he wanted others to know about it because it was so good. Here's the recipe: salted cod fish, cabbage, spring onion, garlic, red chilies, green beans, green peas, curry leaves, oyster sauce, mushroom sauce, soy sauce, rice, eggs. My father is smiling and rubbing his stomach as I write this.

The city buses in Port Louis are not like the ones back home. The drivers decorate them in colorful ways with drawings of flowers and fish. One bus I saw had mermaids on it. The drivers give them names like "Lulu's" or "Sam's Bus" or "Beautiful" or "Groovin.'" I like that because it shows that the drivers take pride in their buses. On our way back to our hotel, the driver had to swerve sometimes to avoid monkeys who would grab things off the road and then dart back into the bushes.

Mauritius feels so far away from the rest of the world, but the children play just like anywhere else. There is also wildlife like other countries—only certain animals are bigger, like the tortoises. They are huge. They are so big that kids can ride on them!

Vietnam

- Vietnam shares a border with three countries. What do you think they are?[4]
- Vietnam is the largest exporter of cashew nuts and black pepper in the world. Too bad I'm allergic to tree nuts.
- Also, many people in Vietnam have pigs as pets instead of dogs. They are called potbelly pigs.
- Vietnam has the world's largest cave, Son Doong.

Everyone rides a moped in Vietnam, often with two or three people at the same time. Sometimes they use their mopeds like cars or trucks. I saw a man on a moped carrying a mattress. Another one was holding a car tire with one hand and driving the moped with the other and had a chicken in a cage on the back.

Crossing the street is dangerous. They teach kids in grade school how to do it because it's an important life lesson in Vietnam. You just have to trust yourself. The thing is, you have to walk slowly forward, always keeping your eyes focused on the driver's eyes coming

4   See the back of the book for answers.

at you. If you stop or walk backwards, you can get hurt. I became good at this. Every time you cross the street in Vietnam, it feels like an accomplishment.

The things I love most about Vietnam are the people and the food, specifically the fruit. People are super friendly and want to help you. They call you "boy." They ask "Everything okay, boy?" or, "You like that food, boy?"

The best fruit is mango, and the Jack Fruit is huge. It's almost the same size as me! We had mango in the Mekong Delta, which my father says is one of the most fertile places on the planet. He says if there was a Noah's Arc of fruit and vegetables, it landed in the Mekong Delta. There was a war here once between the Americans and the Vietnamese. My papa (my father's father) was in it. In fact, my father talked to my papa on a cell phone while we were buying coffee from a lady in a long boat at a floating market in the Mekong Delta. My father explained to his father what he was seeing. It brought back memories for my papa. He was a bit surprised that we were in Vietnam at all.

He told my father a story about when he first arrived there. He was only there a couple of weeks, and a priest asked him to take him up the river in a boat somewhere to say mass. After an hour or so, the priest asked my grandfather if he was lost. My papa didn't want to admit it, but he *was* lost. He had to drive the boat really fast to return down the river. The next day, my papa realized he had been in a neighboring country called Cambodia with the priest. He said that wasn't a good day.

My father ate huge snails in Saigon with a man named Kong. In another part of Vietnam, our hotel had an outside shower. One night when I was getting cleaned up for dinner, I noticed two big snails near my feet the size of golf balls. I was thinking of our home back in Virginia, so I decided to call them George and Martha, after George Washington and his wife.

In Hanoi, we watched people play badminton on the sidewalks at the end of the work day. Everyone plays it there. And when they are done, they sit at cafés and have a drink on little chairs that look like children's furniture. They do that everywhere in Vietnam. People also exercise together in the parks.

Near Danang, my father rented a motorcycle and put me on the back. We rode all day through rice fields and small villages. In one village, we stopped to have something to drink. I had a fruit juice. My father had a beer served by a man with no front teeth who seemed happy to see us. Then we played a little soccer with local kids. They were excited to play with me, and I was excited to play with them. Later that day, the road was blocked because there was a Buddhist funeral. People came from miles around. My father and I couldn't pass, so they told us to come to the funeral. There was incense, and they played a kind of music I've never heard before. It's interesting how people in different countries do funerals.

Thailand

- The ceremonial name for the city of Bangkok is one of the longest names in the world. Want to know what it is?[5]
- They have a fish in Thailand that uses its two front and two back fins to push itself up waterfalls. It can also crawl on land!
- Thailand only has three seasons each year—wet, cool, and hot. It gets six months of rain, three months of cool, and three months of hot.

If you want to be in the biggest water fight you've ever seen, go to Thailand during their New Year festival called *Songkran*. People just throw water on you, even policemen! When we were on a long river boat in Bangkok, an old lady came out of her house and sprayed us with a hose. She thought it was so funny. Later that day, in a colorful tuk tuk, we made a turn down a road, and a huge elephant put his trunk in a barrel of water and sprayed all of us. Elephants are everywhere in Thailand. Then these guys in a pickup truck pulled up next to us and shot us with water guns. My father bought me a water gun the next day, and

5   See the back of the book.

I got into a water fight with a bunch of kids. It was a lot of fun.

Days later, we found ourselves in the middle of the country in a town that had thousands of monkeys that sort of lived side-by-side with the people. Around noon, we were watching people make food offerings to Buddha, who was a religious teacher. I spotted a pack of monkeys sneaking into the top window of a bank. They started wrecking the place. Some men with long wooden sticks showed up in cars. They went into the bank and started hitting the monkeys so they would stop robbing the bank. My father said, "Sam, take note. I'm pretty sure you'll never see anything like this ever again."

People in Thailand love Buddha. There are statues of him all over the country. When you go to Buddhist temples, you can't goof around and act like an idiot. You have to be calm and wear long pants. My father didn't have long pants at one temple, but they gave us some.

Another thing that is different in Thailand than in other places is they are funny about people's heads. It's the most important part of the body to them. You're never supposed to touch someone's head, or they'll get cross—especially the heads of children.

I like the street food in Thailand. They have a lot of things on sticks, including scorpions. No way I ate those, but other people did.

Once a year, there is a festival in Thailand where the people invite monkeys to dinner. They make them rice, fruit, salad, and sometimes ice cream. At the River Kwai, we went to a prison camp where men were forced to build a railroad. They even made a movie out of it. We stayed on a floating hotel. Every time a boat went by, our room rose up and down. It was pretty darn cool. My father ate a fish with a lot of peppers. His face turned red and tears formed in his eyes.

After dinner, a massive thunderstorm came down the river. It felt like we were on a ship. The next day we rode on a train with no glass in the windows through the river valley. The breeze hit us in the face, which was nice because it was so hot. I studied a pretty girl who was younger than me as she looked out the window, and we watched the trees and the valley go by. I wonder what she was thinking.

Bermuda

- Bermuda is only 22 miles long and 1 mile wide.
- John Lennon wrote some of his songs in Bermuda.
- The white roofs on Bermuda homes aren't there to look good, they are to reflect the sun and catch rainwater, which Bermudians store in tanks under their homes.

I have two cousins who are growing up in Bermuda, so I am lucky to visit this beautiful island a lot. In fact, I learned how to walk in Bermuda when I was a baby on—would you believe it—Bermuda grass!

Bermuda is shaped like a fish hook and is part of a volcano in the Atlantic Ocean. The rest of the volcano is underwater, but you can see it from an airplane. The island is 640 miles off the coast of North Carolina.

I love it for many reasons. The air smells like flowers and cedar. The beaches are pink, like the color of those strawberry shortcake ice cream bars on a stick, and the water is see-through. It's blue like the sky, unlike the Potomac, which tends to be brown. All you have to do is put a mask on and look down, and you see all kinds of fish swimming below—angel fish, sergeant majors, wrasses, and parrot fish. You want to know something interesting about parrot fish? If the male dies, the largest lady parrot fish that he hangs out with changes into a male. Bermuda also has some dangerous fish like barracuda and moray eels.

The people in Bermuda are pretty laid back, not like in Washington or Paris. A man named Mr. Davis always picks us up at the airport when we arrive. I love riding with him. He's from Jamaica and has a thick accent. He always seems to be in a good mood. Mr. Davis tells us stories about his life. He's very picky about what he eats, so he only eats fish, rice, and vegetables for dinner with a glass of red wine and a single Scotch Bonnet pepper. He only eats fish that swim in the ocean around Bermuda.

I remember one time driving with Mr. Davis when a storm was blowing into Bermuda. He was listening to an American radio station. The people on the radio were all excited and using scary words like "It's huge," and "Don't go outside," and "It may be the storm of the century."

"American weather stations are always trying to scare you," Mr. Davis said, shaking his head. He switched the dial to a British station, the BBC, and said, "Shall we listen to the real weather?" A British man used language like "Bit of rain, bit of wind, nothing to be particularly bothered about, but take any precautions as necessary." We all laughed.

A few of the things I like doing with my cousins are rock climbing, cave exploring, and cliff jumping. These are all things that we can do to earn points in a club that my father started for us called Young Men of Fire. We have to do things like commit acts of generosity and challenge ourselves with physical tasks.

My cousin, Alex, is particularly good at cliff jumping. He does backflips. A couple of years ago, he was the youngest participant in a cliff diving competition where people come from all over the island. This past year, while we were cliff jumping, we found an old wrecked bike underwater. It looked like it had been there for hundreds of years, but it was probably less.

There's a cove on the island where kids go to play on floating bouncy castles. What I like most there, though, are the green turtles. They don't seem bothered by us. They slowly circle in the water, wondering what we are doing. And when we leave, they're sad. They stick their heads out of the water as if to say, "Don't go yet, we want to continue playing with you."

Washington, D.C., USA

- Not every president has lived in the White House.
- The jazz musician Duke Ellington was from Washington, D.C.
- The National Cathedral has lots of gargoyles. One of them is Darth Vader.

You know how I said earlier that New York is about money, Hollywood is about movies, and Israel is about religion? Well, Washington tends to be about politics. Washington also has a lot of people from the military and people from the technology industry, but politics is still number one.

I live in a town called "Old Town Alexandria." It's just outside of Washington, D.C. It's one of the oldest cities in America. Once upon a time, a lot of tobacco was sent from Alexandria to the rest of the world. A sad part of Alexandria's history is that it was one of the largest slave-trading places in America. There's still a house on Duke Street that was used by a company that bought and sold slaves. Several years ago, while I lived in Paris, they found a slave graveyard under a gas station in Alexandria. They took the station away, and now they have grave sites with a big sculpture.

Many famous leaders from the early days of America used to spend time in Alexandria —people like George Washington, Thomas Jefferson, James Madison, and John Adams. They used to drink beer at a place called Gadsby's Tavern, which is still here. Mount Vernon, George Washington's house, is only a few miles down the road from my house. My father takes me there on weekends. We get there early, just as it opens, when no one else is there so we can say hi to the sheep, the cows, and the pigs. When we leave, we look at the license plates of the cars in the parking lot to count all the states.

We often read in the garden together at Mount Vernon and put our faces in the sun when it's cool in the morning. They have something called an *orangerie*, which is an enclosed brick building where they grow oranges. It reminds me of the Jardin du Luxembourg in Paris, where I used to spend a lot of time. I liked watching old people sit in chairs against the orangery there. They would put their faces in the sun, too. Sometimes they would read newspapers or books. Other times, they just watched people. Old people like those sorts of things.

Robert E. Lee, who was the head general of the South during the American Civil War, grew up in Old Town Alexandria. The town was immediately taken over by northern troops when the war started. One time, the leader of Great Britain, Winston Churchill, visited Alexandria.

One of the things I like most about living in Alexandria is that people are from all over the place. Many have lived overseas at some point in their lives, and they understand what life is like outside of the United States. Washington D.C., where I go to school, is only a few miles away. I like going to the museums and to D.C. United games. There's some cool graffiti in that part of the city.

San Francisco/ Oakland/Yosemite/ Sequoia, USA

- California is home to the biggest trees in the world.
- The grizzly bear is the state animal.
- The fortune cookie was invented in San Francisco.

San Francisco is different from where I live in Virginia. To begin with, it is often foggy. Sometimes when you walk along the street, one side is foggy and on the other is sunny. They call it "microclimates."

The people are different in California. It's hard to say. They are really into what they eat, and everyone seems to walk around with a cup of coffee in their hand.

San Francisco has trolley cars, unlike most American cities. When I lived in Paris, instead of taking cars, I took trains and metros. Not driving cars is more environmentally friendly, and I also think you get around quicker. Many American cities used to have trolley cars, but then they took them away. San Francisco kept theirs and even bought up trolley cars from other cities.

The body of water around San Francisco is the Pacific Ocean. The Pacific is colder, deeper, and bigger than the Atlantic. The water outside of San Francisco bay is full of Great White sharks. They also have huge sea lions. I saw them crawling over each other when we had dinner on the Wharf. They try to push each other off planks of wood, like King of the Mountain.

We went to a book store. The man serving us coffee had a big ring in his nose and tattoos. My uncle Justin was with us. He picked up a book in the shop called *How to Talk to Your Cat About Gun Control*. My father thought it was funny; I didn't really get it. That night, my father bought a big crab from a Chinese fish market, and we ate it on the grill with friends Margot and Lucas. It was sweeter than the crabs we have from the Chesapeake.

We also went to Oakland to see a cousin. We stayed the night in their house, which was built in the 1920s and had impressive woodwork by a man named John, who lived with them. John and my cousin, Ed, taught me how to toss a frisbee for the first time in a nearby park.

We went to Oakland harbor. My father wanted to introduce me to a place that celebrated one of his favorite writers, Jack London. He wrote a book called *White Fang* about a dog in the Yukon during the gold rush. White Fang had a hard life. He survived a famine that killed his brothers and sisters and was forced to fight other dogs until he was saved and moved to California. Also in Oakland, we saw a boat called the *Potomac* that used to belong to President Franklin Roosevelt. He was the U.S. president during the Second World War.

By far my favorite thing in Oakland were the big white cranes on the ship docks. They looked familiar, but I didn't really know why until my cousin told me they were the inspiration for the director of Star Wars to create the white All Terrain Armored Transport (ATAT) vehicles in the movies.

From San Francisco, we made our way to Sequoia National Forest, where the largest living trees in the world live. I saw one tree called General Sherman, which they think is between 2,300 and 2,700 years old. It is almost 300 feet tall and 100 feet around the base. My father and I became official junior park rangers. We had to take a test. I learned a lot about the trees, like the fact that they are very picky about where they live—only between 5,000 feet and 7,000 feet above sea level. And for a tree that size, they don't have a tap root. Their roots are shallow but reach very far. It was peaceful hiking among the sequoias and redwoods.

There was so much snow when we were there that we had to snow shoe. It was my first time. It feels like you're floating on top of the snow. When my father and I looked up at the trees, they seemed to touch the sky, like Jack's beanstalk. I think they must talk to each other up there because they are all by themselves. I wonder what they talk about.

Paris, France

- The Eiffel Tour was only supposed to be temporary.
- There is only one stop sign in the entire city of Paris.
- There is a lake under the Garnier opera house.

I wanted to end our book with Paris because it means a lot to me. I moved there when I was three. In many ways, it is the most difficult chapter to write because I know it so well. Have you ever noticed that it is usually the place where you live that you know the least? I think it's because you aren't looking around or paying attention as closely as a place you are visiting.

But I did pay attention in Paris—it's where I first smelled hot croissants. We lived above a Jewish bakery. Bakers put a lot of butter in croissants to begin with, but this baker put even more—like two sticks!

Paris is where I first learned how to ride a bike. My father used to jog in the gardens of Versailles on weekends. One Saturday he took me and my bike there. I fell down a lot, like kids everywhere. On one tumble,

I remember one of the statues in the garden looking at me. It was like he was saying, "Stop messing up my garden." I know it sounds fancy to say that you learned how to ride a bike in the gardens of Versailles, but for me, it's just where it happened.

Paris is also where I heard different languages for the first time—French, Arabic, Spanish, Portuguese, Russian—you name it. It's where I learned the difference between cheeses made from a cow and those made from a sheep. It's where I heard people sing sad songs in the metro with an accordion. It's where my dad once made a child's car seat for me with a wooden wine crate. It worked well.

Paris is where I learned about paintings. My father would play a game with me at the Louvre or the Musée d'Orsay. He would take my friends and me into different rooms and have us try to find certain things in the paintings like a dog, a hammer, or a treasure. I liked playing this game best with my friend, Agata. Paris is where I learned how to ride a push scooter and read a metro map and play boules in the park.

Paris is the first place I tasted wine. It was at something called the Salon d'Agriculture. It happens once a year in February. The Presidents of France always show up to kiss the cows and pigs. If they miss it, French people get upset with them. The Salon d'Agriculture takes place in a huge exhibition hall at Port de Versailles. Farmers and wine and cheese makers come from all over France to sell their stuff. It's like taking a holiday to France, but all in one building. You can just walk around and tour different regions of the country. One year my mother and father were tasting wines from a part of the country called Burgundy. The wine maker pointed at me and said, "Why don't we let him taste it?" My parents said, "Sure." The man asked, "Do you know why I want him to taste it?" My parents shook their heads. "Because children's tongues have not been injured." My parents looked confused. "They've never had their tongues burned, and they've never smoked a cigarette or eaten too much salt—all the things that kill a tongue. Children can taste things in the wine that adults can't." So, I tasted the wine. The man looked curious. "So, what do you think?" I don't remember what I said, but my father reminds me that I said something like, "Chocolate, dirt, and smoke." "Bravo," the man said, "Bravo."

Paris is where I learned how to play soccer (or football to my non-American friends). My favorite places to play were the Jardin du Ranelagh and the Champs de Mars, but I would play anywhere. Paris is where I first went to school. It's where I remember my early birthday parties with friends. It's where I learned how to order my food in a different language.

I miss Paris and the life that we had there, like falling asleep looking at the top of the Eiffel Tower. But I like where we live now. Every place has rich people and poor people. Every place has people who work and play and laugh and cry. Every place can be the best and the worst at the same time. Every place has children.

I feel lucky that I know Paris as well as I do. It's something no one can ever take away from me. I hope you have things like that in your life.

Answers

Belgium:

Q. How many countries border Belgium?

A. Four: The Netherlands, France, Germany, and Luxembourg.

Italy:

Q. Tomatoes weren't originally from Italy. Can you guess where they were from?

A. No one, single country. They came from the Andes mountains in South America, where they grew wild in places that are now the countries of Peru, Bolivia, Chile, and Ecuador. They were first cultivated by the Aztecs and the Incas.

Vietnam:

Q. Which countries border Vietnam?

A. China, Laos, and Cambodia.

Thailand:

Q. What is the ceremonial name for Bangkok?

A. Krungthepmahanakhon Amonrattanakosin Mahintharayutthaya Mahadilokphop Noppharatratchathaniburirom Udomratchaniwetmahasathan Amonphimanawatansathit Sakkathattiyawitsanukamprasit.

Conclusion

I hope you've enjoyed our book. We tried to give you an idea of what other places are like—countries and cities both far away, and maybe even close to your home. There are a lot of cities and countries that we didn't include. There wasn't enough space. Maybe next time. I still want to spend time in a lot of places in my life. I'd like to visit Indonesia to see the Komodo Dragon; or Tokyo because they have fancy toilets; or Iceland to see the geysers. I hope I get there. I hope you do, too.

About the Authors

Sam Morrison is half British-half American. He lives in Washington, D.C., is just beginning to understand American football, thinks treacle pudding should be served with every meal, and doesn't understand why old, Italian men pull their pants up so high on their waists. He grew up playing soccer in the parks of Paris and can hold his breath underwater for 25 seconds.

Angus Morrison is Sam's dad. He has spent half of his career in Europe and half of it in the US. He likes good coffee, a well-made martini, and toast. He wishes more people were curious about the world around them and thinks cities should provide advice kiosks manned by out-of-work philosophy students.

Check out Sam's adventures on Instagram at **@samrmorrison**. He wants to hear about *your* adventures. Feel free to send him images of graffiti and street art that you have seen when traveling or even in your own town. Let him know what you were thinking and feeling.